I Am a Little Chef

Mayumi Oono

The chef's kitchen. It's easy to use and clean!

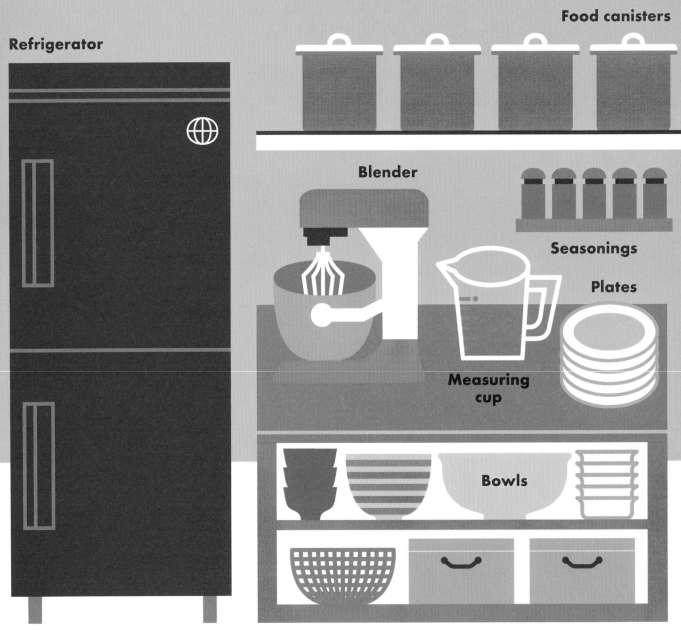

Refrigerator

Food canisters

Blender

Seasonings

Plates

Measuring cup

Bowls

Strainer

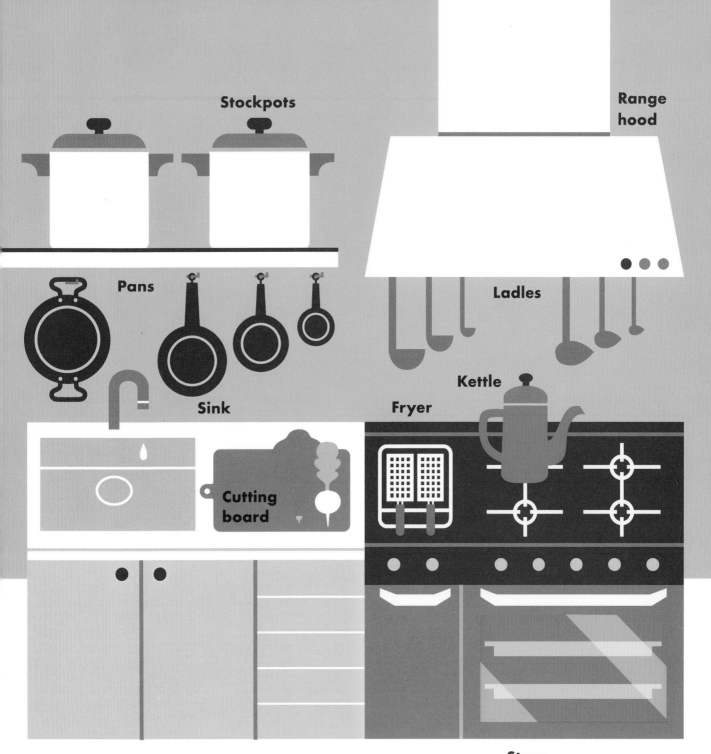

Stockpots

Range hood

Pans

Ladles

Sink

Kettle

Fryer

Cutting board

Stove

The chef's tools. They are needed for cooking.

Tongs

Turner

Ladle

Skimmer

Spatula

Wooden spatula

Whisks

Pizza cutter

Grater

Scissors

Pepper mill

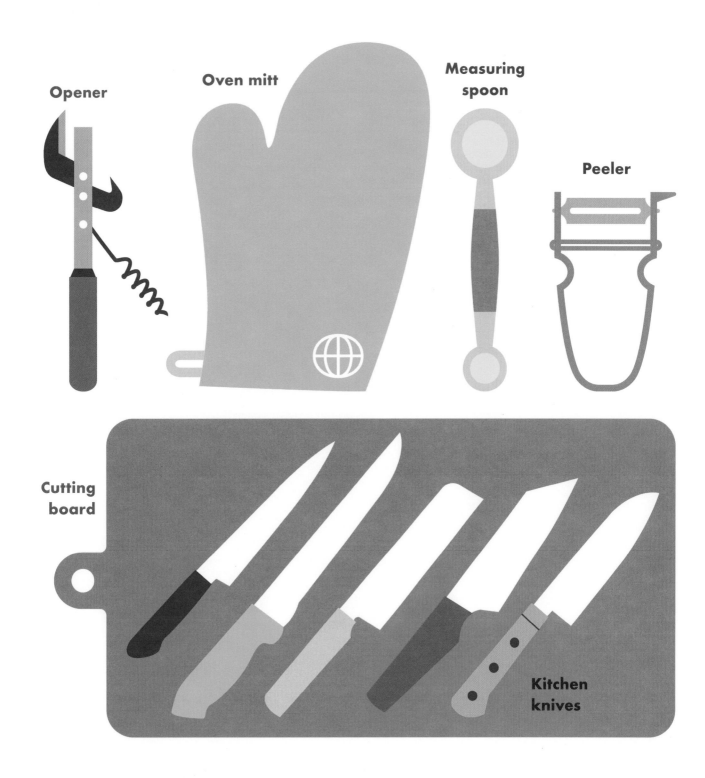

Opener

Oven mitt

Measuring spoon

Peeler

Cutting board

Kitchen knives

The ingredients are very good! Wonderful!

Eggs

Seafood

Meat

Sausages

Butter

Flour

Milk

Bread

Rice

French bread

Apple

Orange

Lemon

Kiwi

Strawberry

Pear

Let's cut some fruit! It is all delicious!

Cabbage

Tomato

Green pepper

Avocado

Onion

Squash

Next comes vegetables. When they are cut, you can see many interesting patterns!

Apple

Orange

Lemon

Strawberry

Kiwi

Pear

The fruit is so fresh! And so shiny! Excellent!

The chef plans the menu and then cooks the food.

Stir-frying

Heat the pan.
Stir-fry the spinach.

Baking

Turn on the oven.
Bake a cake, a pie, or bread.

Grilling

Place the grill over the fire.
Brown the steak.

Boiling

Boil the water in a pot.
Cook the pasta!

The chef uses a variety of cooking methods.

Deep frying

Use heated oil.
Fry the potatoes.

Simmering

Heat a pot.
Make soups and tomato sauce.

Dressing

Combine oil and vinegar.
Use for a salad!

Steaming

Heat vegetables with steam.
It's a healthy cooking method!

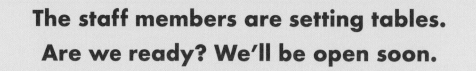

The staff members are setting tables.
Are we ready? We'll be open soon.

Our guests are here.
Welcome to "WORLD Restaurant"!

OPEN
WORLD Restaurant

What will you eat today? The chef will take you on a journey of foods from around the world.

Orders!
OMELETTE, BURGER, PIZZA, and SUSHI... Coming right up!

Use these...

Spinach **Mushroom** **Eggs** **Salt** **Cherry tomato** **Butter** **Pepper** **Carrot** **Ketchup**

The omelette is ready. Bon appétit!

Use these...

Lettuce   **Bun**   **Sliced Cheese**   **Hamburger**   **Avocado**   **Onion**   **Tomato**

The burger is ready. Enjoy your meal!

Use these...

Tomatoes   Basil   Shredded cheese   Olives   Pepperoni   Flour   Olive oil

The pizza is ready. Buon appetito!

Use these...

Tuna

Salmon

Squid

Vinegar

Eggs

Seaweed

Sugar

Rice

Salt

Shrimp

The sushi is ready. We hope you like it!

Bon appétit!

4. Goulash (Hungary)   5. Tacos (Mexico)   6. Veal Milanese (Italy)

1. Xiaolongbao (China)   2. Pho Bo (Vietnam)   3. Scotch Eggs (United Kingdom)

The food is delicious!
Many thanks to the chef!

Next, the chef cooks for a large group of guests!

10. Curry (India) 11. Paella (Spain) 12. Pasteis de Bacalhau (Portugal)

7. Meatballs (Sweden)   8. Galette (France)   9. Fresh Spring Rolls (Thailand)

Special thanks to Mutty (mutty.it).—M.O.

Little Professionals: I Am a Little Chef first published
in the United States by Tra Publishing 2023.

Printed and bound in China
ISBN: 978-1-7353115-5-5

Look for these previously published titles in the *Little Professionals* series:
I Am a Little Fashion Designer
I Am a Little Pastry Chef

Little Professionals: I Am a Little Chef is printed on Forest Stewardship
Council certified paper from well-managed forests. Tra Publishing
is committed to sustainability in its materials and practices.

MIX
Paper from
responsible sources
FSC® C102842
FSC
www.fsc.org

Tra Publishing
245 NE 37th Street
Miami, FL 33137
trapublishing.com

[T] tra.publishing

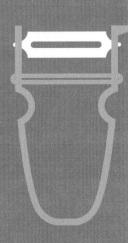

Now do it yourself!